CARVING THE ELK

Dale Power

Text written with
and photography by
Jeffrey B. Snyder

Schiffer Publishing Ltd

77 Lower Valley Road, Atglen, PA 19310

Printed in China.
ISBN: 0-88740-566-5
We are interested in hearing from authors with book ideas on
related topics.

Designed by Mark S. Balbach

Published by Schiffer Publishing Ltd.
77 Lower Valley Road
Atglen, PA 19310
Please write for a free catalog.
This book may be purchased from the publisher.
Please include $2.95 postage.
Try your bookstore first.

Contents

Introduction

The elk, some people hunt them, others shoot them with a camera, I carve them out of wood. For some time now, my students have been after me to create a pattern of an elk that would be both realistic and simple to carve. As you follow the simple instructions in this book, I hope you'll agree that I have succeeded.

Second largest of the deer family, the elk, or Wapiti as the Native Americans called them, are found mainly in mountainous pastures or wooded terrain in the Western United States today. Originally they were plains animals but were killed in great numbers by the cattlemen trying to protect their grazing lands.

Tan in color with a yellowish rump patch and tail, the male has a dark brown mane on his neck and throat which distinguishes him from the female when he sheds his multi-tined antlers. The males also stand about five foot tall at the shoulders and weigh nearly eleven hundred pounds when mature. In spite of their large size, elk can run at impressive speeds of up to thirty-five miles an hour and are also excellent swimmers. So you can see why I carve them instead of trying to run after them!

My elk is carved out of Basswood, also known as American Linden, because of the forgiving nature of the wood as well as the high quality and durability of the final product. Basswood is classified as a hardwood, but I find it great for either hand or machine carving.

While we're speaking of carving, I used a bench knife, a set of assorted hand gouges, an Optima-1 Wood Burning System, an Optima-2 high speed grinder and assorted carbide burrs for this project. The paints used are acrylic washes.

When you use power tools, it's always wise to protect your lungs with a dust mask or dust collection system like the one you'll notice in the photographs.

Thus prepared, I hope you'll enjoy the book and have as much fun carving your elk as I've had carving mine.

Carving the Elk

Pattern reduced **75%**.
Enlarge **133%** for original size.

To follow Dale step by step through the book, proceed from the upper left, down the left column, then to the upper right and down the right column. It's just like reading a newspaper.

To begin, the elk will be carved from three layers of 3/4 inch basswood glued together with waterproof yellow carpenters glue. This cuts down on the carving time. Transfer the pattern to the 3/4 inch basswood boards.

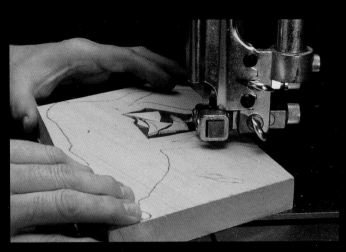

Cut the pattern out of the basswood. Don't forget to cut the ear out at the same time.

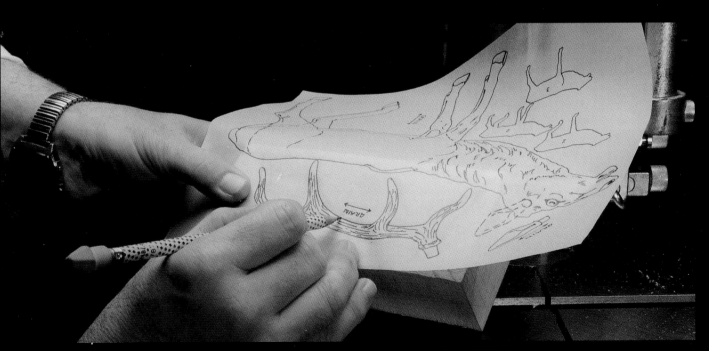

Transfer the pattern for the elks' horns onto the side and top of a 2x3x7 inch piece of basswood. This is the size you need to cut out both horns from the same piece of wood. It keeps the horns symmetrical. Note that on the drawing the grain direction is mark for the strength of the antlers.

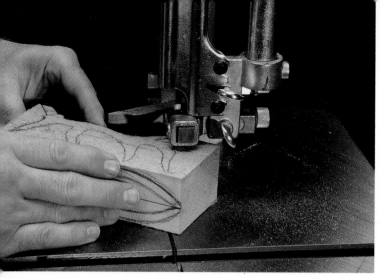

Keeping your fingers well away from the saw blade, cut out the side profile of the antlers. Save the wood cut from the bottom of the antler to provide a base to hold the antler upright while cutting the upper profile of the horn.

You will need the guide drawn in the top to cut the rest of the antler.

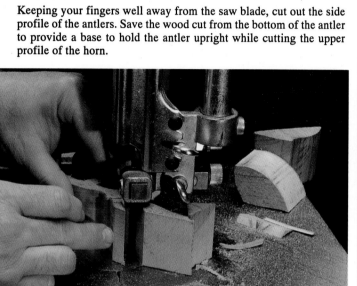

Clean up the little details.

Prior to cutting out the top view of the horn, reassemble the top and bottom pieces you have cut off. Keep your fingers out of the holes in the antlers or you will injure yourself. It is wise to plug these holes for safety's sake.

Do not cut through the top of the wood block.

The blade should be set 1/8 inch higher than the wood to make sure the blade holds steady. Cut along the guide on top of the wood block.

The first horn is falling away from the block.

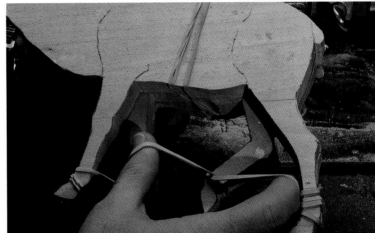

After cutting the pieces of the elks' body out, glue them together with yellow carpenter's glue and clamp them tightly with rubber bands or wood clamps. The glue should be allowed to set for 24 hours. It forms itself into a resin which is not water soluable but which requires time to set.

Following the guide lines, you will end up with a right and left hand version of the horn.

Always draw a center line on your piece before starting to carve. It is easier to do it now while you have square edges. Animals are basically symmetrical and you want a center line to keep your animal in proportion on both sides. Draw the center line all the way around, allowing you to balance your pieces from any point.

Take a measurement of the length of the head.

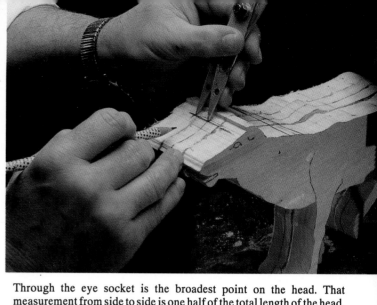

Through the eye socket is the broadest point on the head. That measurement from side to side is one half of the total length of the head. Mark those spots on the head.

Transfer the head measurement onto a piece of paper and divide it into 1/8 inch segments.

The next point will be where the neck meets the shoulder, and it is three quarters of the length of the head.

To draw the dorsal (back) view of the animal, you measure off the center line at 90 degrees beginning with the nose. The width of the nose is one quarter of the length of the head.

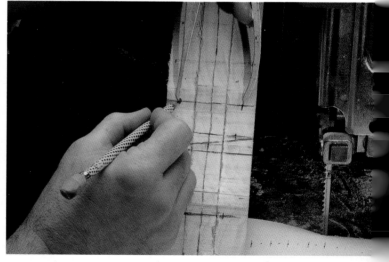

Moving down the back, the broadest point of the shoulders measures 7/8 of the length of the head.

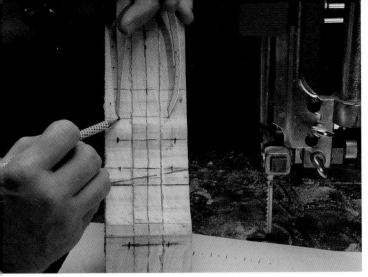

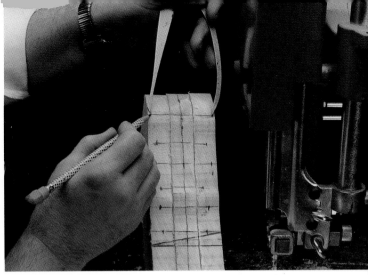

This is followed by the point right behind the front shoulders. It is 3/4 of the length of the head.

Through the hips is the broadest point of all, measuring 1 1/8 the length of the head.

The next measurement is through the stomach area. It is one full head in length.

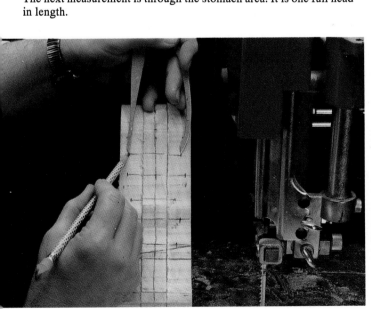

Just in front of the rear flanks, the measurement is 7/8 of the length of the head.

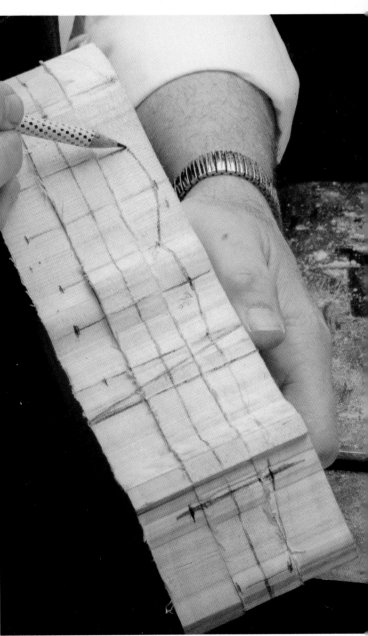

Now you get to play connect the dots.

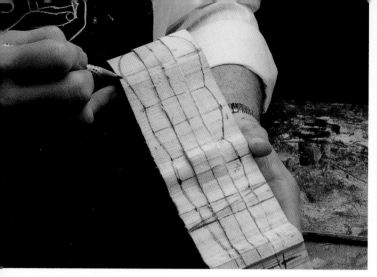

This is the final drawing of the dorsal view of the elk.

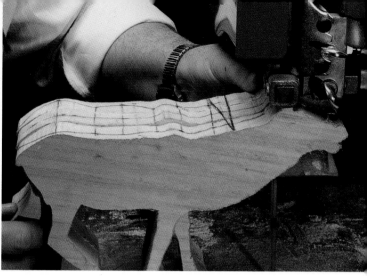

Follow the new dorsal guide lines and cut away the excess wood. Stay on the outside of those lines. You can always carve back to them but you can't add wood back on. Once again, keep your fingers along the side of the animal and not in the leg openings underneath to prevent cutting your fingers.

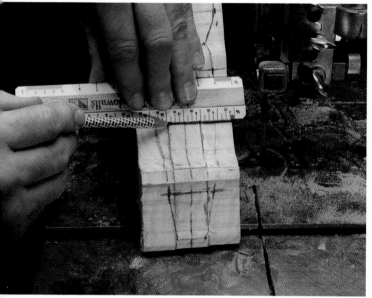

If you choose to turn the head, now is the time to decide how far to turn it. This decision is made by first drawing a straight line about half way between the head and the shoulders or roughly one head length back from the ears and approximately two head lengths back to the shoulders.

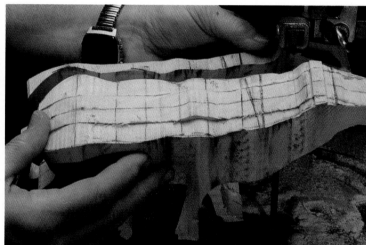

Now you have the animal pretty well roughed out in the dorsal view.

Now draw roughly a 30 degree angle.

The next thing we are going to do is cut his head off. Keep the first cut as straight as you can for centering.

10

Next cut the 30 degree angle on the neck.

Take wire brads, cut off their heads, and place two along the center line on the head portion of the elk. Keeping the outer edge of the body aligned, the brads will line up along the center line of the body and provide additional support when you glue.

As you can see, the turn of the head is now made. Further cuts may be made to steepen the angle of the turn but be careful not to cut off the front hoof.

Push the head and body together without glue first. This allows you to check for fit.

Complete a center line on both the head and the body portion throughout the cut.

Spread a thin layer of carpenter's glue on the head portion.

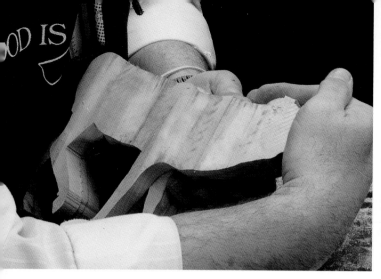

Press the head and body together and wipe off the excess glue that squeezes out of the joint at this time.

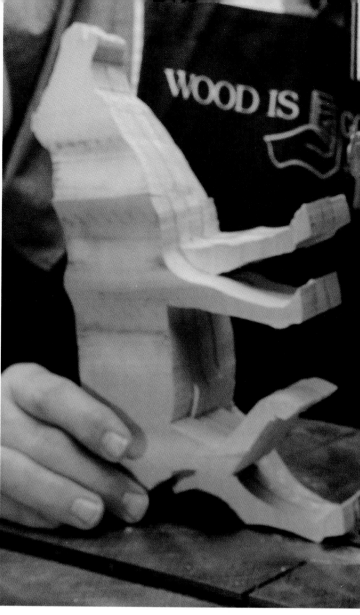

Wipe off the excess glue.

Using a band or a coping saw, cut the center line up the legs of the elk to the base of the belly. Be careful or the legs may snap off.

The head is now secured in place with rubber bands. Set your elk aside to cure for 24 hours.

If a leg should break off ...

... hold the pieces together and draw a match line along the side of both pieces that will help you fit the leg back together in proper alignment.

The carpenter's glue protruding from the crack is useful in this case. Take sawdust and sprinkle it over the glue, rub it in with your finger and you will create a wood filler that plugs any irregularities which may show. This insures a nice smooth joint.

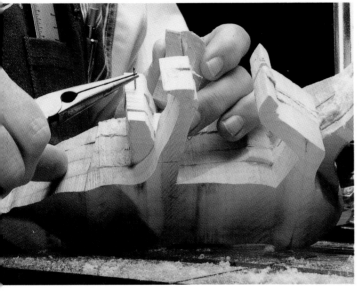

Cut the head off a brad and force the pointed end into the upper portion of the leg. Make sure the brad is centered in the leg where it will be out of the way and will not damage your cutting tools later on.

Apply yellow carpenter's glue to the lower section of the leg and then fit the leg in place over the pin until it abuts with the upper leg. An exact match of the leg is not absolutely necessary as you will be reducing the size of the leg later.

Now round the corners off all around the upper back with the band saw.

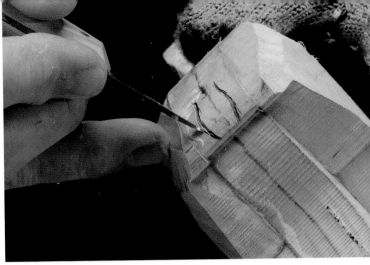

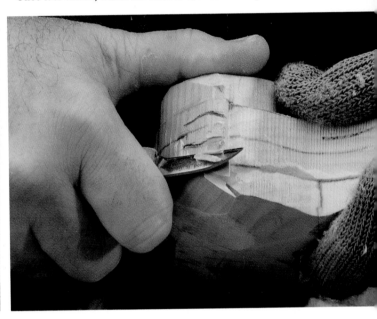

Round off under the neck. The rest the band saw will not reach. Make sure always to keep your fingers well away from the exposed blade. Also make sure to keep fingers out of the gaps between the legs.

Round off back to the incised tail. Carve in from both sides of the tail. You should wear a carver's safety glove like this one to avoid the chance that a slipping blade will cut you. You will not round off the legs until last. The legs are the weakest point and the most likely points you will grip while carving elsewhere. Avoid holding them while carving to avoid snapping them off, carved or not.

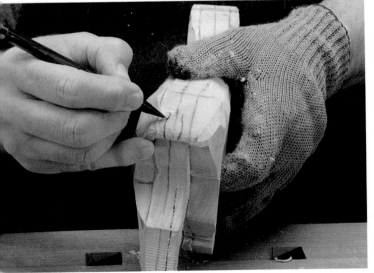

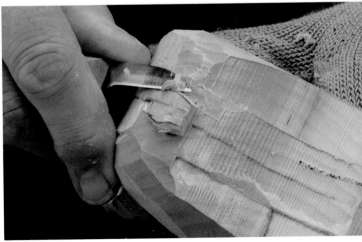

Now sketch the tail in with a pencil.

The rounded off area around the tail should look like this.

14

The tail should stick out this far from the rump.

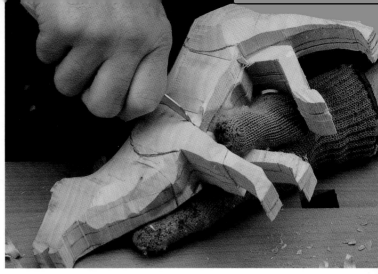

Incise the shoulder, elbow and hip marks with a bench knife to about 1/16 of an inch deep to act as a stop cut.

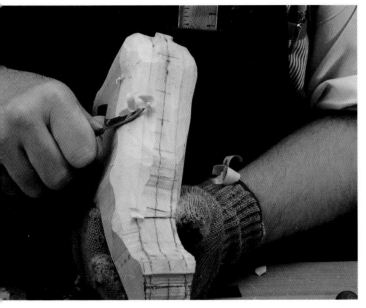

Round down the back from the center line down over the sides.

Mark the side center line on the both sides of the elk.

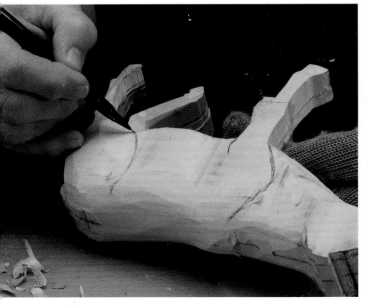

Mark on the locations of the shoulder, elbow and the hip in pencil.

Round down the stomach area between the elbow and the hip cut line down to the center line of the belly.

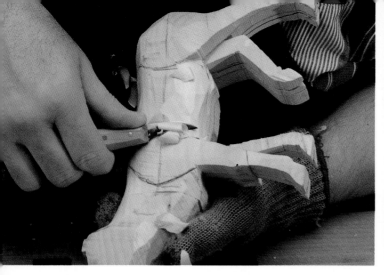

Continue rounding the belly up to the center line on the side of the elk.

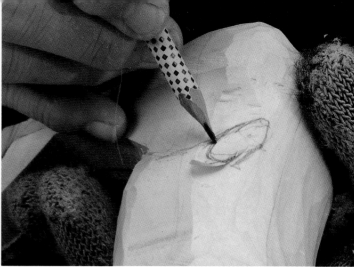

There is quite a hollow around the top of the forward facing rear leg because the leg is pushing up against the ribcage, forming this space.

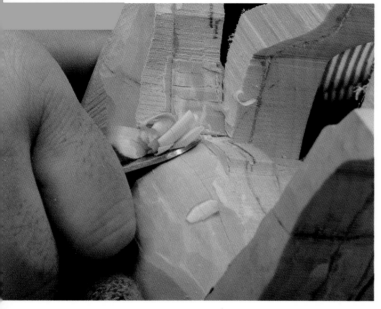

Continue rounding up the back legs.

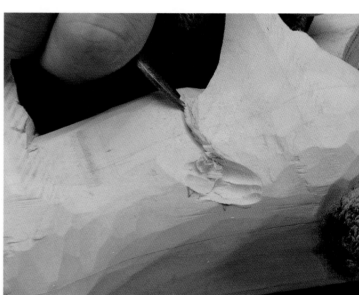

Rough out the hollow and inscribe the front leading edge of the rear flank with a bench knife.

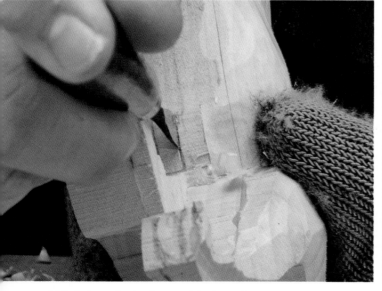

This being a buck, draw and incise a line along both sides of his genitalia.

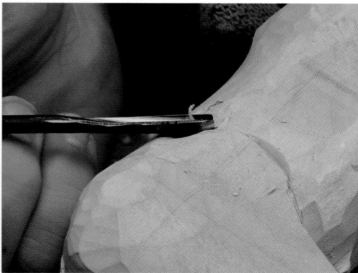

Take a couple of cuts with a U shaped gouge to refine the hollow and the deep line down the leading edge of the rear flank.

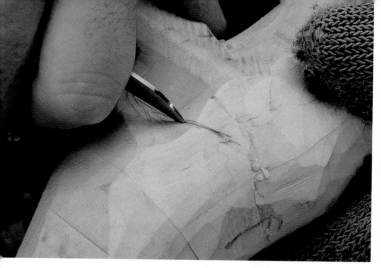

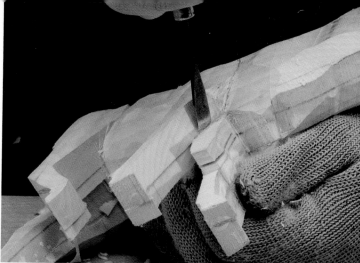

Now incise the cut line along the leading edge of the front shoulder with a bench knife.

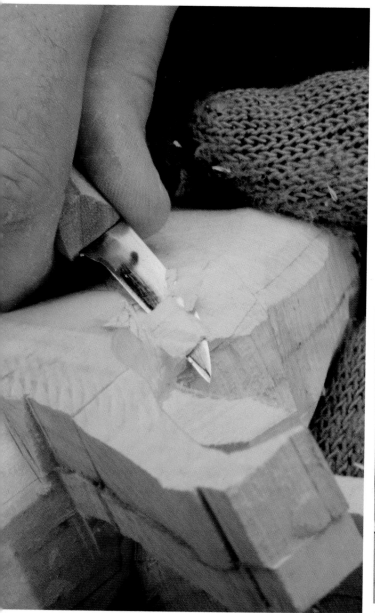

Carve back to the cut line to remove some of the wood.

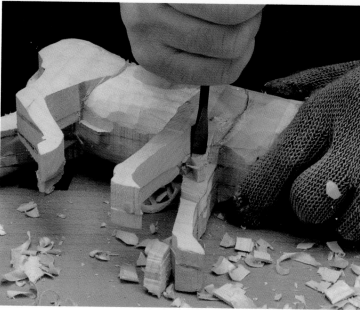

At this time remove the excess wood from in between the legs with a square gouge. Work slowly in this area. Make sure you cut clean and don't take a chance in breaking a leg off.

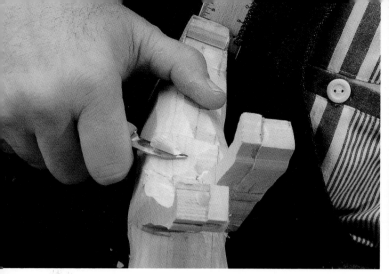

Now you are free to work in the area between the legs, rounding down the extra stock with a bench knife.

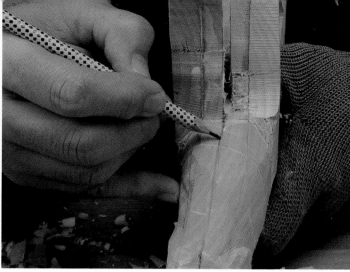

Once the neck is rounded, refresh your center line. As you remove material on either side now, leave the center line high in a rounded point. This will create the dewlap.

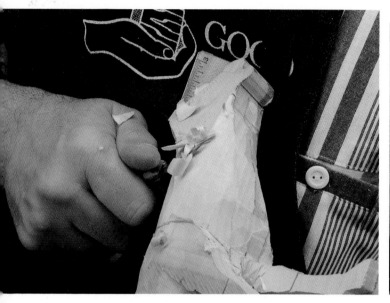

Continue by rounding the neck.

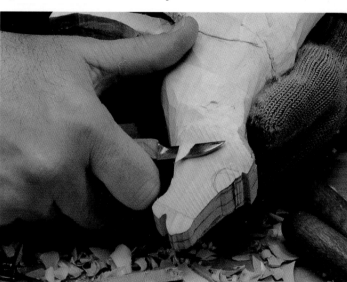

Now, the back of the jawline has to be carved down slightly so that it can be blended into the neck.

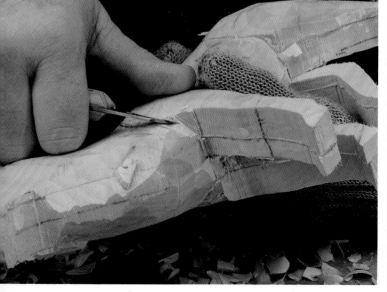

Clear off in front of the shoulder as well, allowing for the dewlap which goes between the front legs.

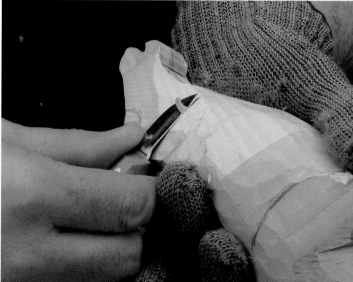

Here is the blended jawline.

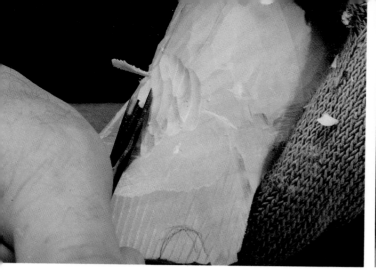

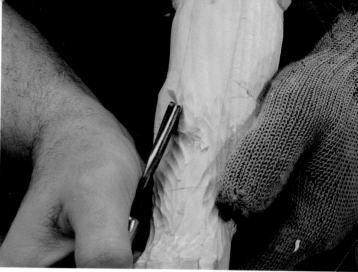

At this point, take a U shaped gouge and carve in the ruff on the neck. Take care to leave the higher center line down the underside center of the neck to form the dewlap.

Take the ruff up on top of the hump above the shoulders with your U shaped gouge.

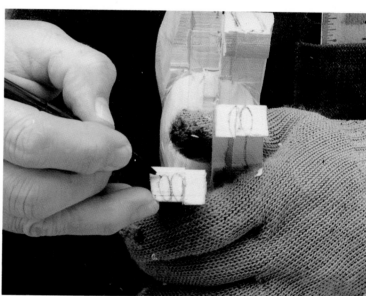

Here is the dewlap.

Draw the hooves on the base of the elk's feet.

Carve the dewlap up to the center line on the upper side of the neck. The ruff should be carved in the direction water would run around and down the neck.

The width of the foot is the same as that of the knee.

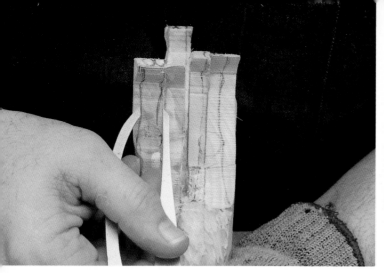

The lower leg is 2/3 the width of the foot.

Shape the hoof down with a square gouge. Make sure to support the hoof with your thumb or you will snap it off during shaping.

The upper leg where it joins the body is 1 1/4 the width of the foot.

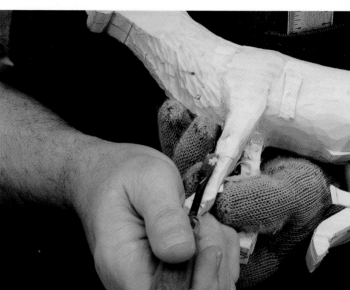

Now work your way up the leg, roughly shaping it while remembering to leave enough wood for the dewclaws on the backs of all four legs. Always work from the hoof up, being careful not to pry on the leg.

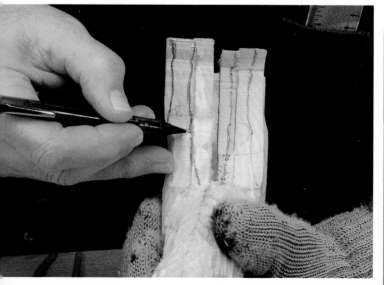

Now draw in the legs. I realize that in real life the lower leg is far thinner than I have indicated, but for the stability of the leg I have increased it in size.

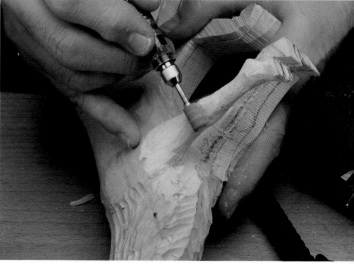

Once you have the leg roughly shaped, finish working down the leg with a drum shaped kutzall on a power grinder.

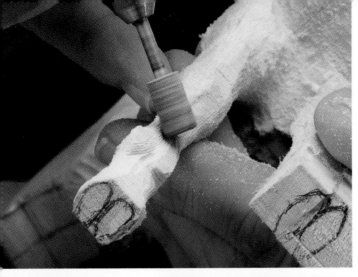

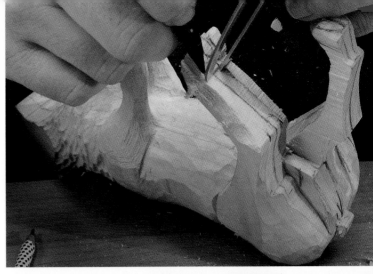

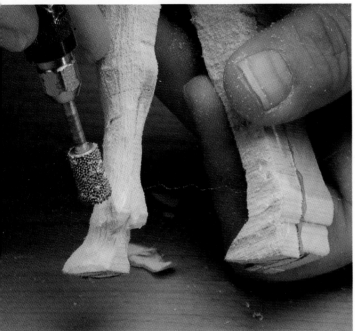

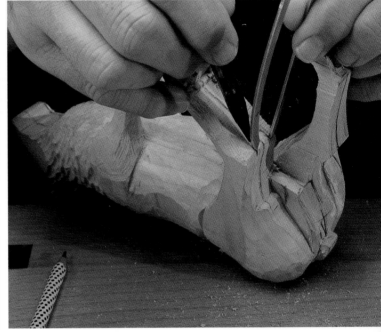

Here is the dewclaw you remembered to leave enough wood for.

Measure and mark the size of the hoof, fetlock and ankle symetrically along the leg, following the centerline.

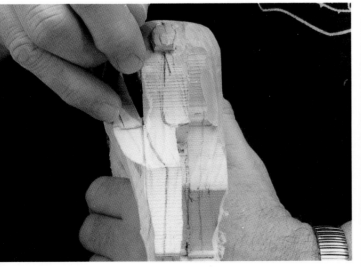

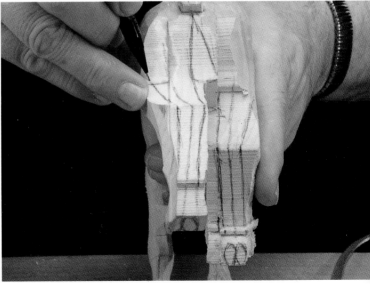

To draw the back legs, remember that the hoof, fetlock and the ankle are all the same size. Draw a single line down what you believe to be the center of the leg. If you are unsure about the basic shape of the back leg, go look at a cow.

Draw in the leg like this.

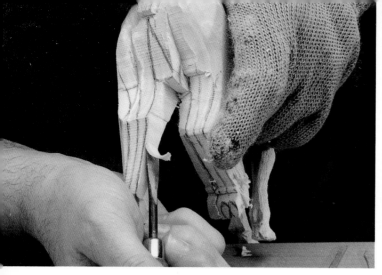

Reduce the rear legs, being careful to leave enough room for the dewclaws and between the rear legs for the scrotum. Here a square gouge is being used.

The drum kutzall in the high speed grinder also works well for defining the hoof.

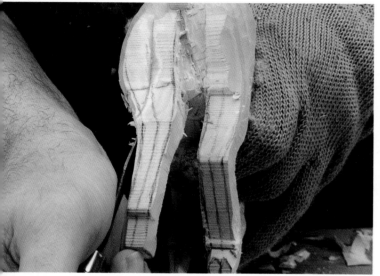

Keep reducing the rear legs. Note the dewclaw.

Here is how the shaped rear leg should look.

Using the drum kutzall in the high speed grinder makes quick work of the leg reduction and shaping.

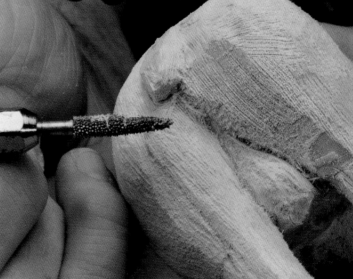

A cone shaped kutzall works well for shaping the scrotum. Here is how the shaped scrotum should look.

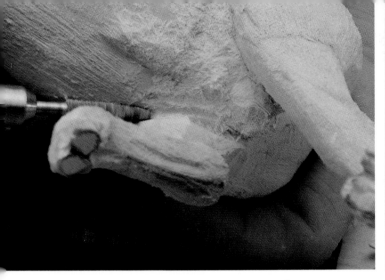

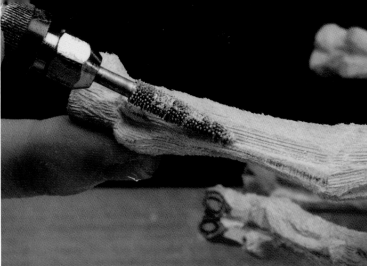

Cut deeply along the inner edge of the raised rear leg with the cone shaped kutzall so that it appears free from the rest of the body.

Put in the achielles tendon along the rear lower leg with a cone shaped kutzall. Remember to support the leg with the thumb of your other hand while you cut.

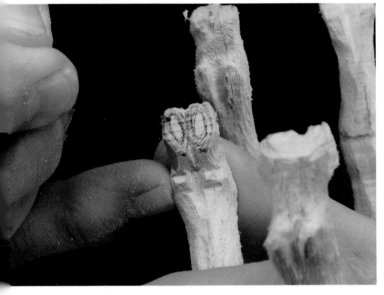

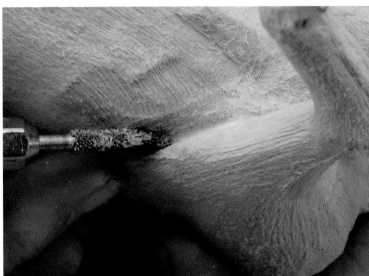

The upraised hind hoof requires special attention. The bottom must be hollowed out except around the very edge to 3/32 of an inch.

Cut deeply along the inner edge of the raised leg to show separation from the body with a cone shaped kutzall.

Create the hollows at the base of the upraised rear hoof with a cone shaped kutzall.

The achielles tendon extends up the inside of the upper half of the rear legs as well and is detailed with the cone shaped kutzall.

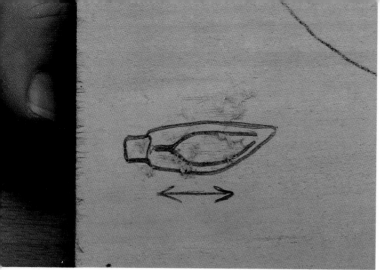

Draw the pattern of the elk's ear on one of the three pattern blocks now. The block is thick enough to create both ears from the same piece of wood. The arrow reminds you to draw the ears following the wood grain, running the grain along the length of the ear for strength.

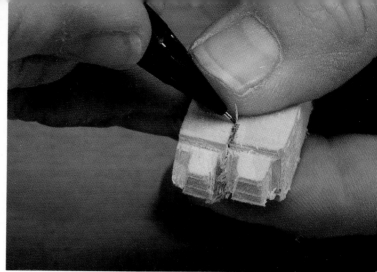

Now mark the center line.

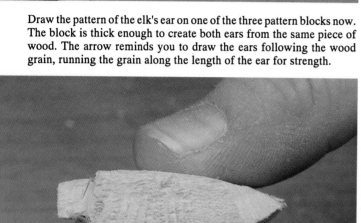

Using the band saw, cut out the elk's ears from the pattern block.

Saw the ears apart down the center line running with the grain to form the two ears you need for the elk. Remember, you need to have the grain run from the tip to the bottom of each ear, keeping the ears from becoming fragile because of cross grain.

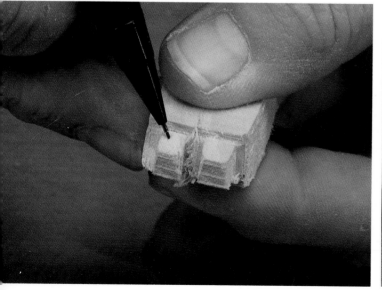

Then shape the tenons with the band saw, being very careful to keep your fingers away from the blade.

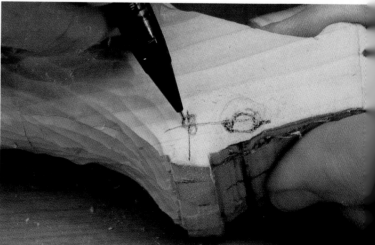

The ears are located directly below the point where the horns will connect to the head and behind the eye on the same level as the eye.

24

Once you cut the pattern in half, there is a definite right and left ear.
Mark the inside of each ear on the rough stock.

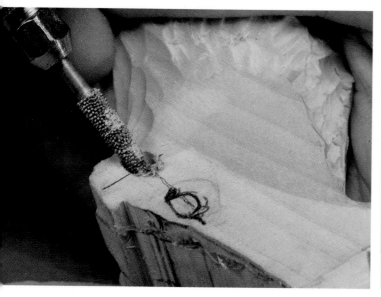

Angle whatever you use to drill the ear hole from the back to the front
to get the proper angle for the attitude you want to project with the ears
of your whistling elk. Used here was the cone shaped kutzall.

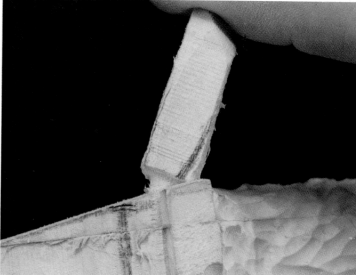

Now draw a guide line in that will help you to shape the back of each
ear to fit tight against the back of the head.

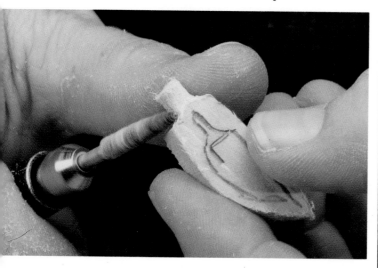

Shape the tenon joints of both ears round to fit in the hole. Used here
was the cone shaped kutzall again. The tenons should be large enough
to fit snugly in the hole.

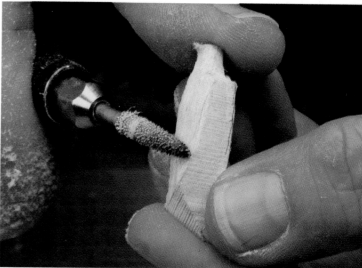

Shape the back of the ear itself. Used here is a cone shaped kutzall. The
front will be shaped later after each ear has been put into place.

See how the shaped back of the ear fits against the head?

Fit the ear into the hole.

Here are both of the roughed ears in place ready to be glued with yellow carpenter's glue.

Sprinkle sawdust liberally over the excess glue to act as a filler to cover the gaps around the ear.

Dip the tenon in the yellow carpenter's glue.

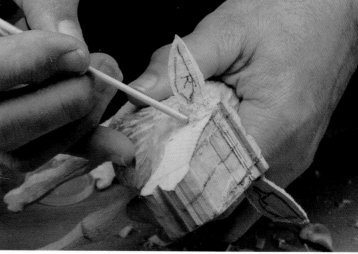

Pack in the sawdust until the glue will hold no more. At this time any slight adjustments to the ears may be made before the ears have set. You need to decide on the look you want: inquisitive, angry, etc.

WE HOPE THAT YOU ENJOY THIS BOOK . . . and that it will occupy a proud place in your library. We would like to keep you informed about other publications from Schiffer Publishing Ltd.

TITLE OF BOOK: _____

☐ hardcover
☐ paperback

☐ Bought at: _____
☐ Received as gift

COMMENTS: _____
_____

☐ *Please send me a free Schiffer Arts, Antiques & Collectibles catalog.*

☐ *Please send me a free Schiffer Woodcarving, Woodworking & Crafts catalog*

☐ *Please send me a free Schiffer Military /Aviation History catalog*

☐ *Please send me a free Whitford Press Mind, Body & Spirit and Donning Pictorials & Cookbooks catalog.*

Name _____

Address _____

City _____ State _____ Zip _____

SCHIFFER BOOKS ARE CURRENTLY AVAILABLE FROM YOUR BOOKSELLER

Now the ears are in place, the gaps are filled and they are ready to dry. Leave the ears to set for at least an hour.

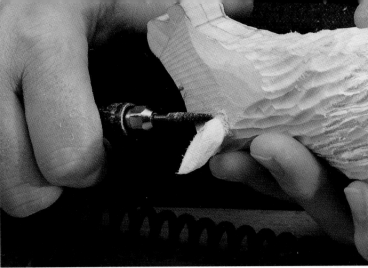

Clean the excess glue and sawdust off around the ears as you go.

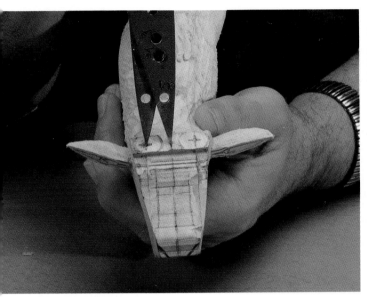

Locate where the horns will be placed. They should be roughly 2/3 of the way out from the centerline.

As you reduce the ear, even though the grain runs lengthwise through the ear, you must support the ear from behind while you reduce it.

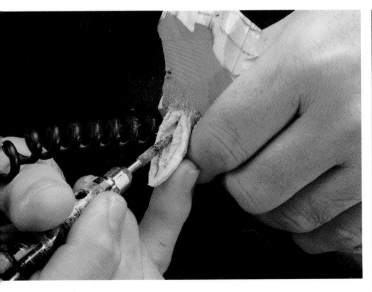

Now go back and use a cone shaped kutzall to cut out and shape the insides of the ears.

Here is how the reduced ear should look.

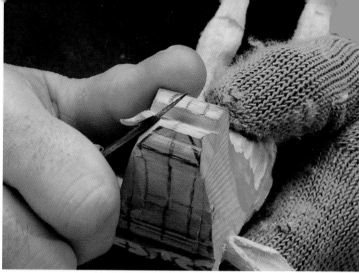

Although the ear appears delicate when the inner edges are shaped, there is still a good deal of wood left to support it. The leading edge of the ear is thin but the rest is left quite thick.

Using a bench knife, cut the angle laid out for the nostrils.

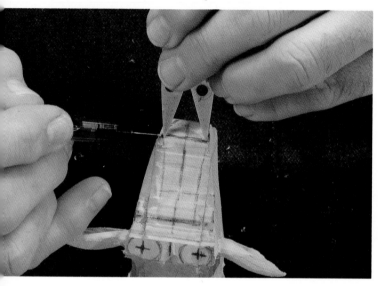

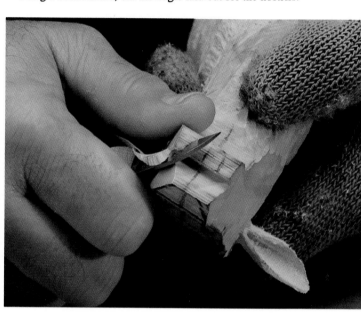

The crest of the nose is 1/2 the width of the head at the eyesockets.

Continue the same angle down to create the proper shape for the lower jaw.

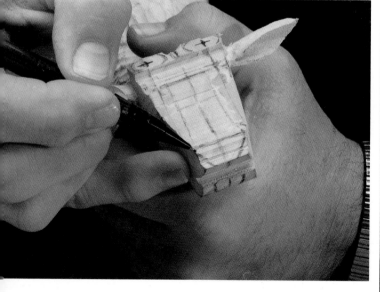

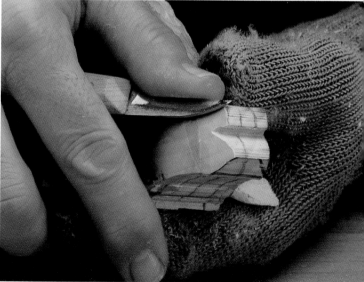

Draw a line to indicate the angle at which the nostrils will be cut. The tip of the nose is half of the width of the crest of the nose.

See how the same angle is followed all the way down.

28

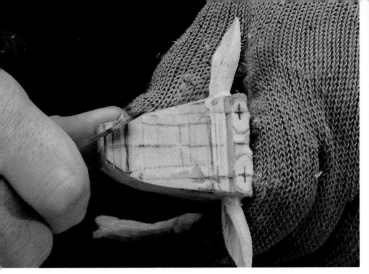

Repeat the same cut on the other side of the nose.

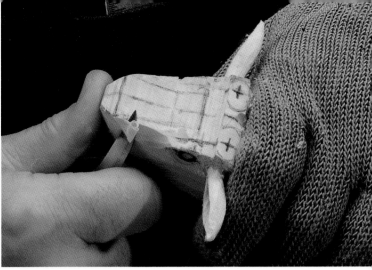

Start rounding the square corners off both sides of the face in front of the eyes and towards the nose.

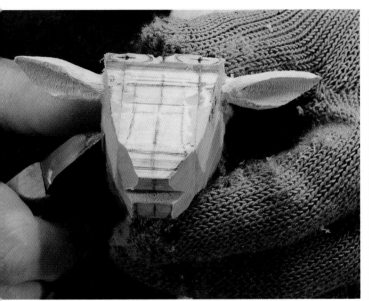

Now both sides of the nose and the lower jaws are reduced.

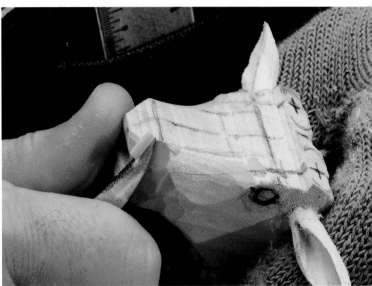

While rounding, make another cut to flatten an area for the nostril openings.

The eyeball itself should now be indicated by an approximately 1/4 inch circle. Draw in guidelines to ensure you leave enough wood for the eyes while rounding down the face.

Round down the lower jaw as well.

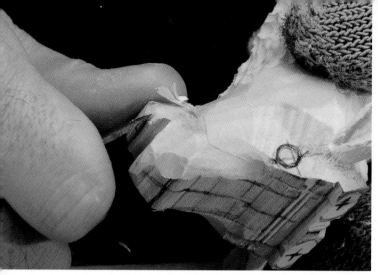

Take off the square corners around the lower jaw.

You can see here how to approach removing stock from below the eye socket.

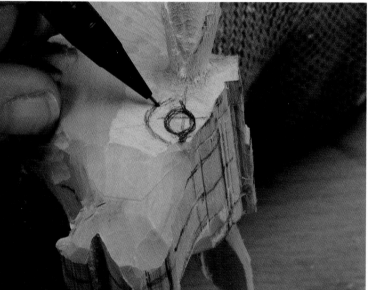

Round the face but be careful to leave an extra orb below the eye for the protruding eye socket below the eye.

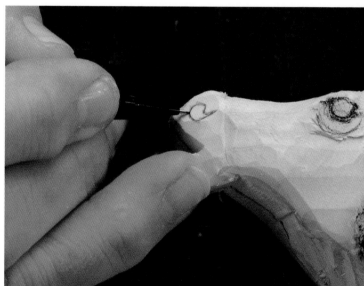

The nostrils are shaped like commas. Draw in nostril guide lines now.

Reduce the area of the side of the face below the eyesocket and back to the jawline.

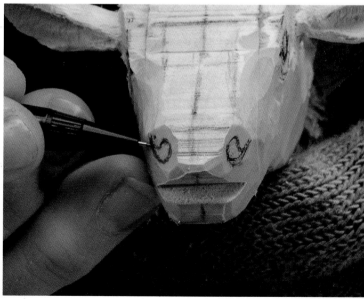

Here are both nostrils drawn in place in preparation for carving.

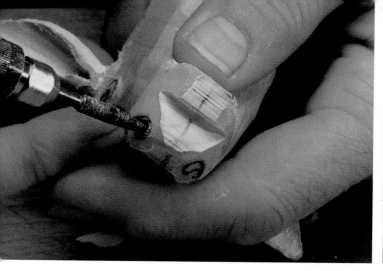

Cut the nostrils in to a depth that looks good to you. Used here is a cone shaped kutzall.

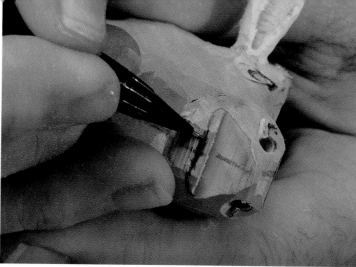

Draw in the bottom lip

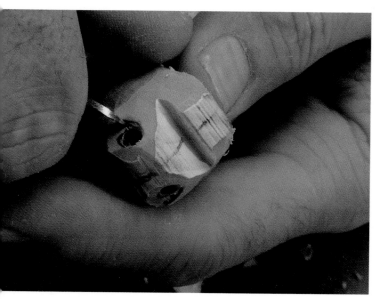

Incise the top line of the nostril with a bench knife.

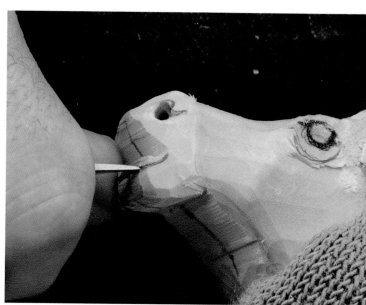

Incise the line for the bottom lip approximately 1/16 of an inch in.

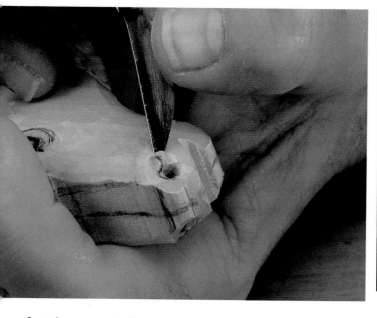

Just trim out a small sliver for the underside of the edge of the nostril.

Remove the front wood down to the incised line for the lower lip to reveal the it.

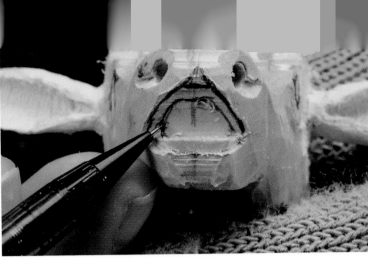

Complete the removal of the wood in front of the lower lip.

Here is how the drawing should look.

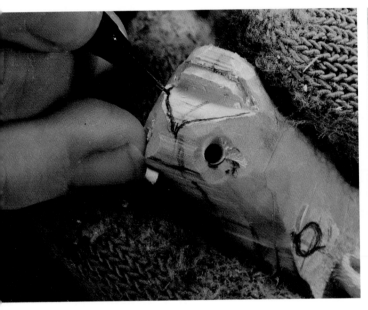

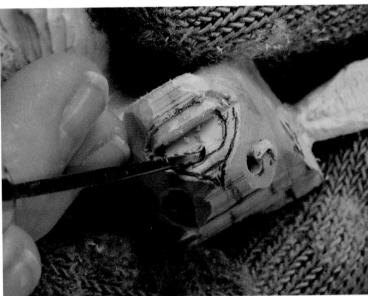

An elks upper lip is split apart in the center. Draw the inner line of the upper lip, exposing this separation.

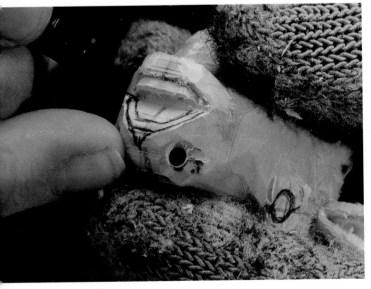

Now sketch the inner line of the hard palate.

You have your choice in cleaning out the roof of the mouth. You can either use a power grinder with a cone shaped kutzall or a small U gouge. If you use the power grinder be careful not to grind away the elk's lower teeth.

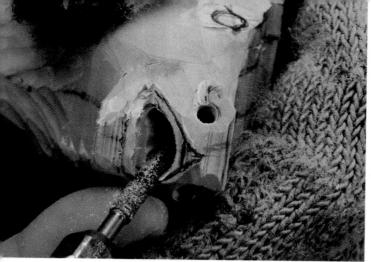

Here is the hollowed out mouth.

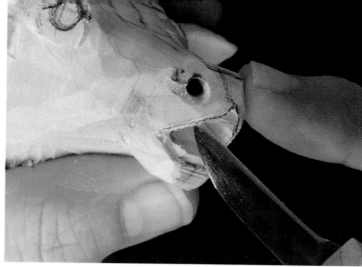

Incise the inside of the upper lip with the bench knife. This will allow you to trim away some material to form the hard palate along the upper jaw.

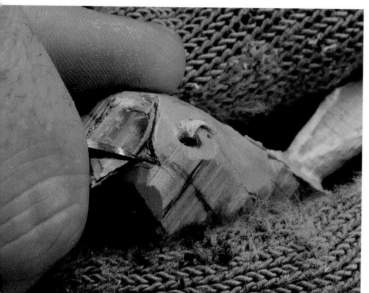

Incise the line of the upper lip with a bench knife.

Trim off the excess material to form the hard palate.

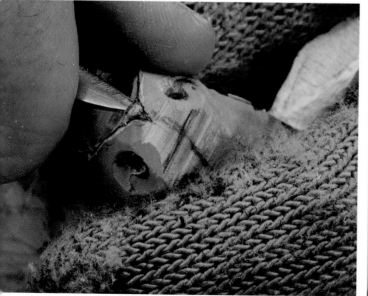

Remove the chip from the separation in the center of the upper lip.

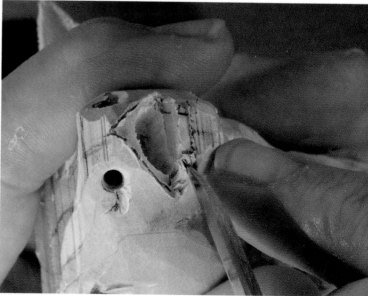

Trim some of the material from the area of the tongue.

33

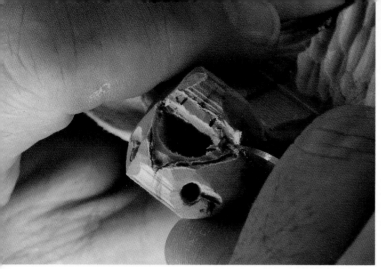

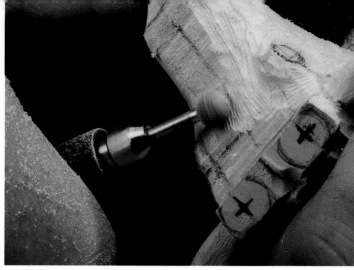

Remove the excess material.

You will also shape down the area between the eyes with the small ball shaped kutzall.

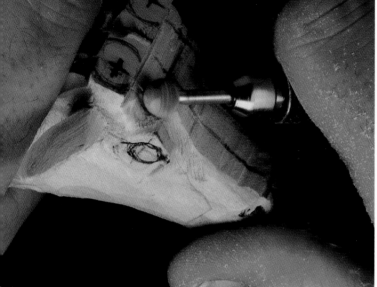

Shape the face over the eyes using a very small ball shaped kutzall.

Also shape the bridge of the nose at this time with the ball shaped kutzall.

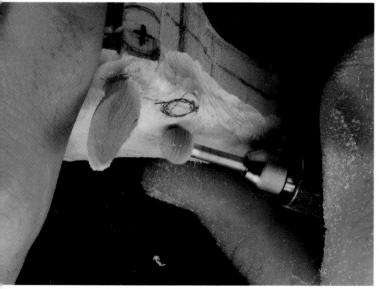

You may reduce the area beneath the eyes with the small ball shaped kutzall as well.

Continue to shape down around the face with the small ball shaped kutzall.

34

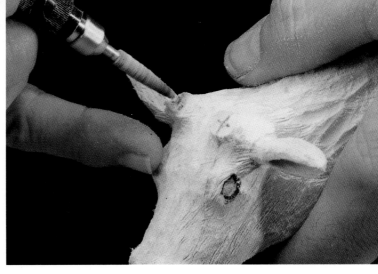

Now drill in the holes to hold the elk's antlers. Work them in as straight as possible. The hole size will be adjusted later to fit the size of the tang you leave on the base of the horn. These holes are being drilled with a small cone shaped kutzall.

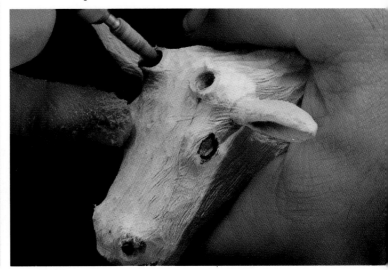

Here are the rough shaped holes.

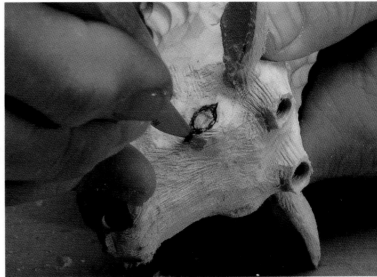

Shape for the base of the horns.

Now you have the shaped head and it is time to shape the eyes.
To cut the eye, first cut the top lid in by placing the bench knife in the corner of the eye at the tearduct, and put a single cut in towards the eye.

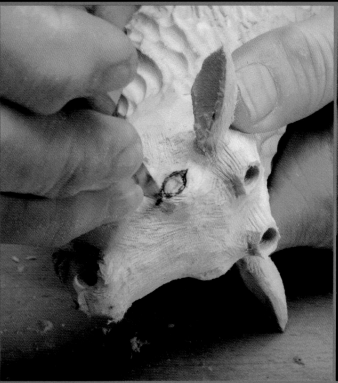

Repeat the same process for the lower lid.

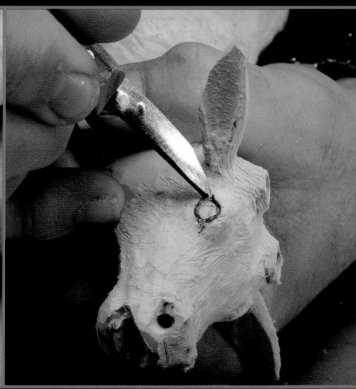

The same process is repeated in the back corner of the eye.

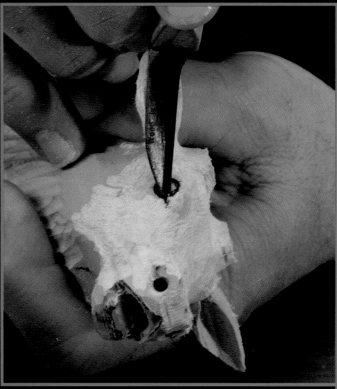

Then cut along the eyeball with your knife facing toward the tear duct, removing a small chip from the corner of the eye.

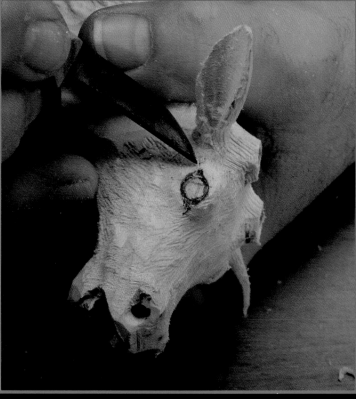

Both chips have been removed.

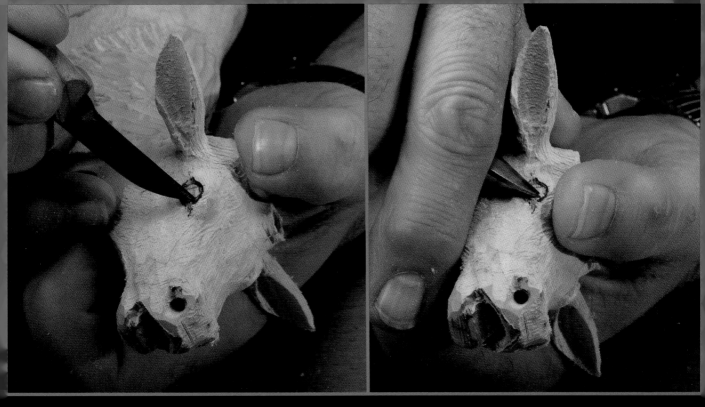

Sloping the knife in an upward position, we will plunge the tip in along the line that forms the upper lid of the eye.

Remove a very small sliver off the edge of the eyeball, both top and bottom. This will give the appearance that the eyeball is beneath the lid. The sliver is very fine.

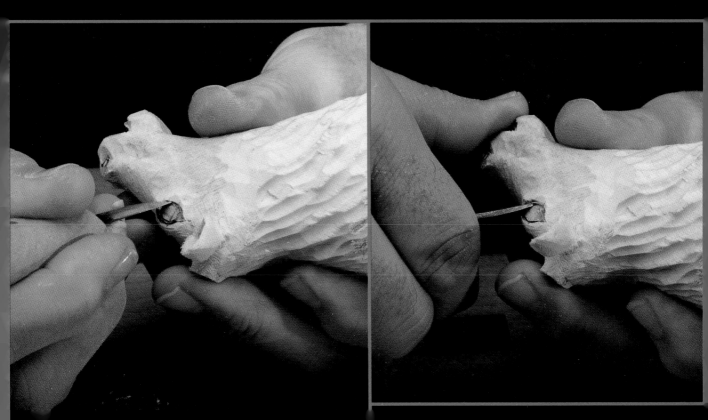

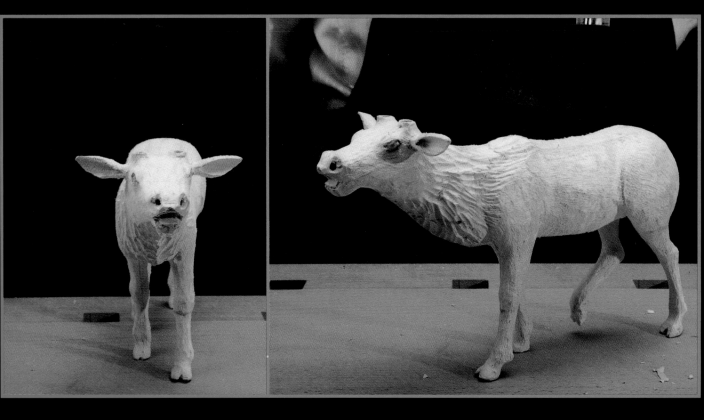

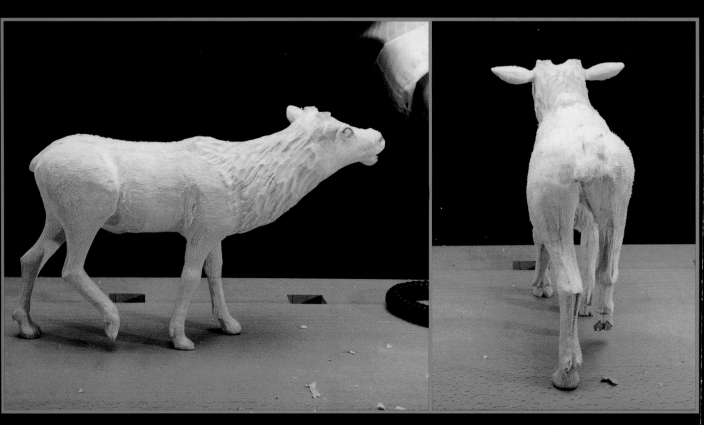

Now we are ready to set the elk aside to await sanding and turn our attention to his antlers.

Carving the Antlers

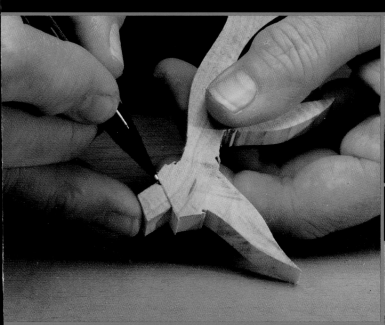

Draw a line to indicate the tenon at the base of the antler.

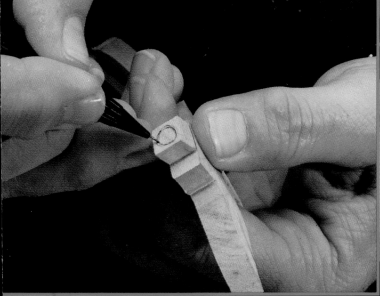

Draw a guideline on the base of the tenon to indicate the size it should be reduced to.

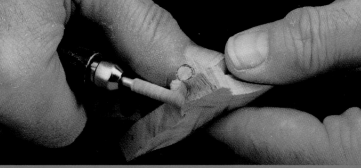

Round the tenon with a cylinder kutzall. Work around the tennon to form a circular shaft.

Now the tenon is rounded.

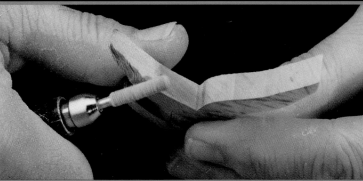

Once finished with this process, we now turn our attention to the tines of the antler. Start working at the tip of the farthest one out and work your way in, rounding the tines with the cylinder kutzall. Always work in from the tip to the shaft of the antler to lessen your chance of breakage.

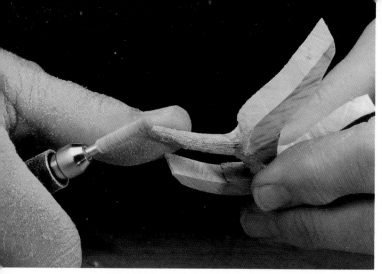

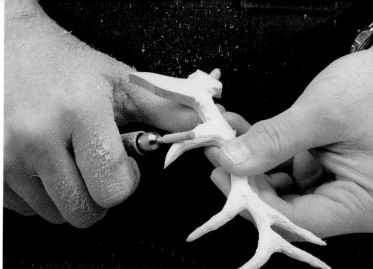

Round the tine down but do not sharpen the tip too much or it will get caught and break.

Continue to work your way to the shaft of the horn. Some of the thinning down to be done will be accomplished by sanding.

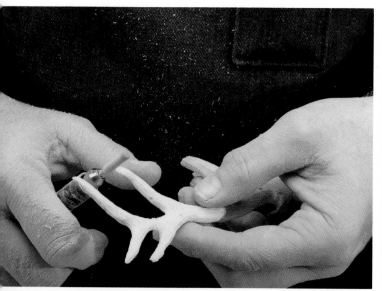

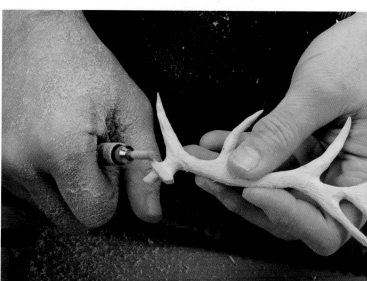

Continue shaping down to the base of the antler.

Continue to round the tines down.

Round off the base above the tenon to form the butt of the horn.

This is how the shaped down butt of the antler should look.

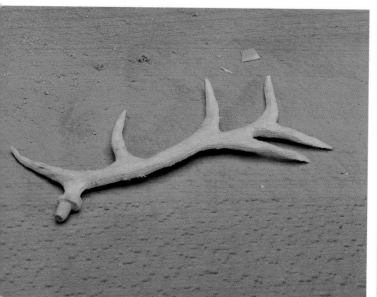

At this stage we are ready to sand the horn down to its final shape.

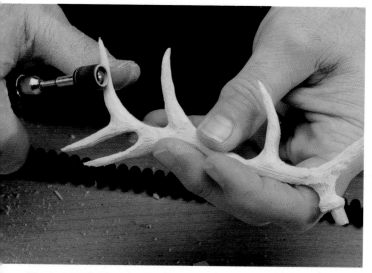

You can sand the antlers by hand if you are very careful not to apply much pressure. It is better to use a small drum sander on a power grinder as shown here. Make sure to keep your thumb under the piece you are working on to avoid snapping the tine off.

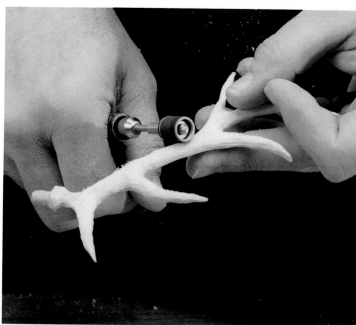

Continue sanding until you reach the desired shape. Don't get discouraged if you break the first set of horns. It takes practice to remember to support the horns you are working on.

Here is the finished antler.

Burning the Elk

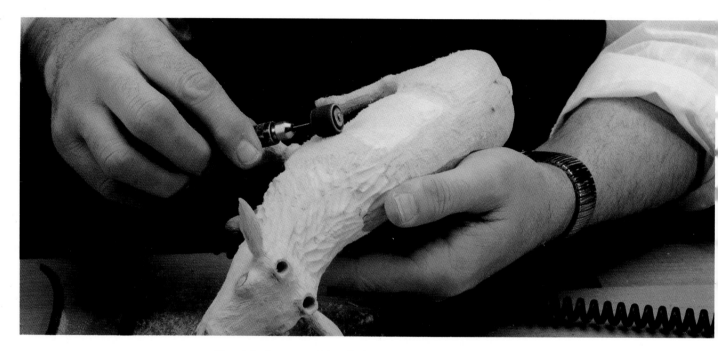

Now it is time to sand the elk. Use a moderate size drum sander.

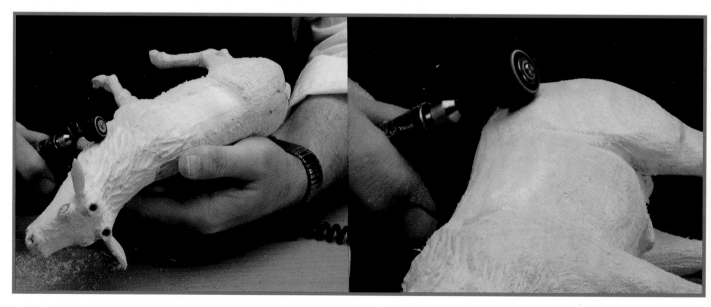

You sand over the ruff lightly to smooth the sharp corners left by your chisel cuts.

Sand the elk smooth, removing the fuzzy surfaces in preparation for wood burning.

42

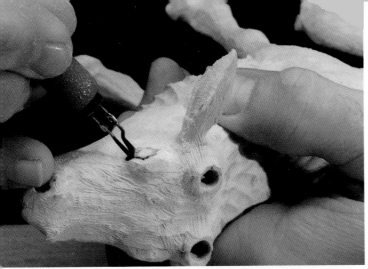

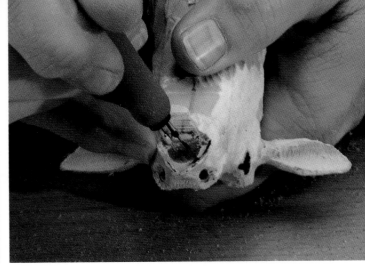

Now on to the mouth. First burn in the line of the upper lip.

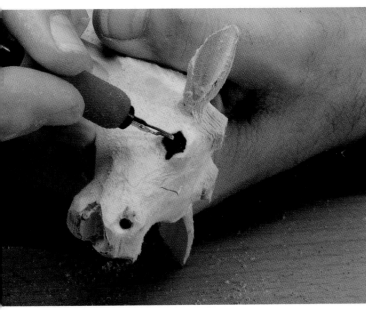

Burn in the previously cut eye lines.

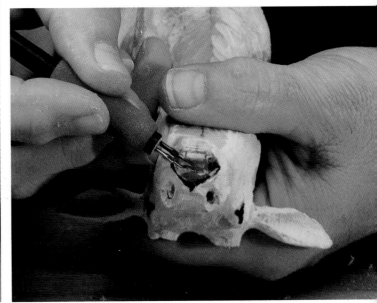

Darken in the hard palate next.

Burn in the eye ball itself to provide color.

Darken the lower lip.

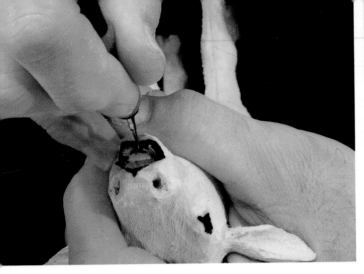

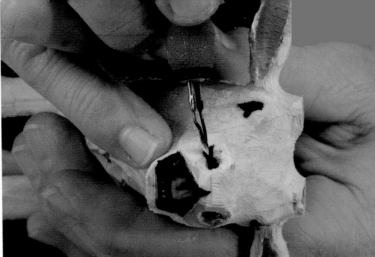

Define the lower teeth by burning in a series of vertical lines to create an even number of teeth (either four or six).

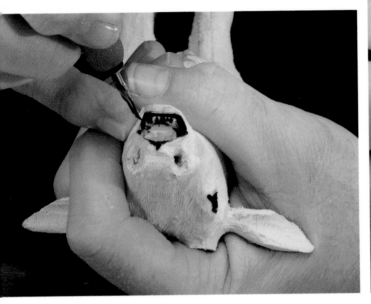

Burn in on the sides within the mouth to represent the tongue.

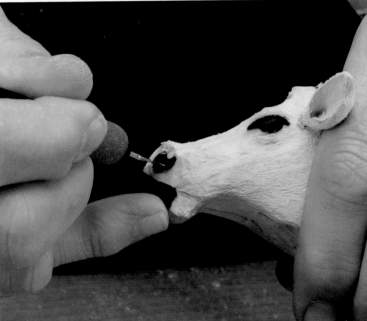

Now burn in the deep inner center of the nostril.

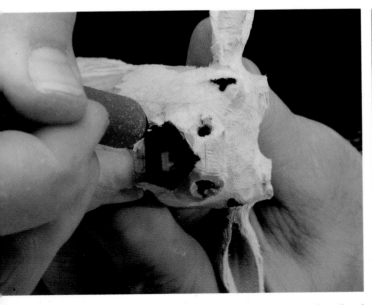

Move on to the nostrils, darkening in the line of the outer edge of each nostril first.

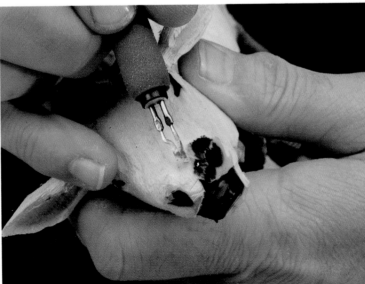

Now darken the area of the exposed skin of the nose by laying the wood burner flat and using it like a paint brush.

Now start burning in the hair from the nose out. Use short strokes for the whole face, making sure they are random and do not line up.

The hair runs straight up to the edge of the horns.

The hair originates in the center of the forehead between the eyes in a swirl similar to the one on top of the human head.

The hair runs out the ears in smaller and smaller strokes as it gets out to the ends.

Continue to burn in the hair on the face.

Leave a small unburned area around the upper eye lid. This area will be white. The hair is too fine to show at this scale.

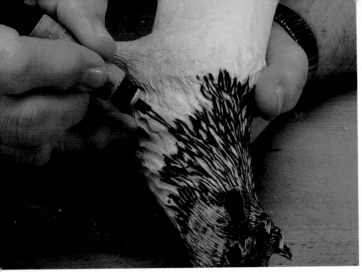

Finish the face out with short random strokes, running the hair up the sockets for the horn. Once you get down onto the neck where the ruff begins, the pattern changes to longer lines following the chisel marks to give a matted look to the neck.

Darken the hooves on all four legs using the side of the burning pen.

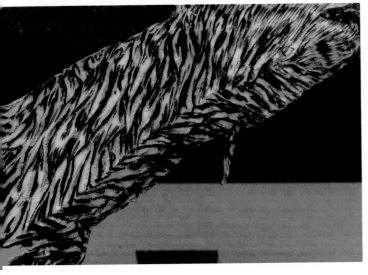

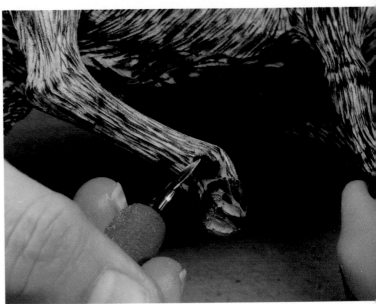

After the ruff, the hair covering the rest of the body is burned on in short random patterns, remembering the pattern is as if a drop of water has run down the animals side from the middle of his back.

Darken the dewclaws with the side of the burning pen as well.

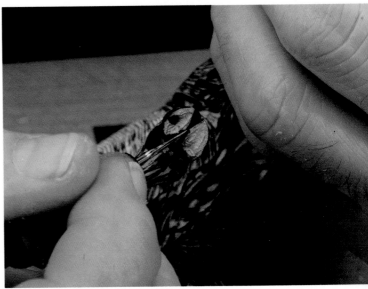

Remember that the ruff travels completely down between the front legs.

On the hind foot that is not touching the ground, be sure to burn between the hooves to show a separation.

46

The Antlers

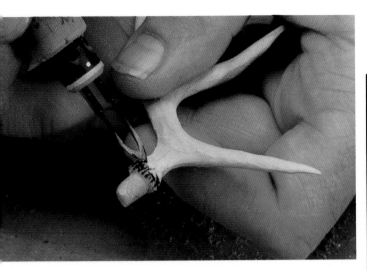

Moving on to the horns, put random depth marks at the base of each horn to simulate the bumps at the base of the horn.

Continue up the tines to the end.

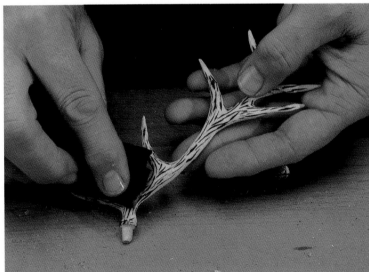

After burning in the lines on the horn, lightly sand with 320 sand paper, being careful not to remove all your lines. Some of the lines will disappear partially, forming random patterns.

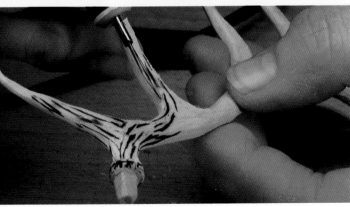

Now burn in random lines of random depths up from the base of the horn, following the length of the horn to show the remains of blood vessels which ran through when the horns were in velvet. The marks always run towards the tips of the horns.

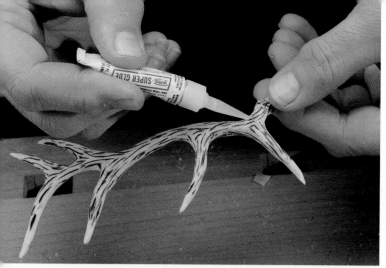

Lightly sand both antlers.

Starting at the base and working out to the tips of the antlers, spread Super Glue over the entire surface in a fine coat. This will aid in the strength of the antlers after they have dried.

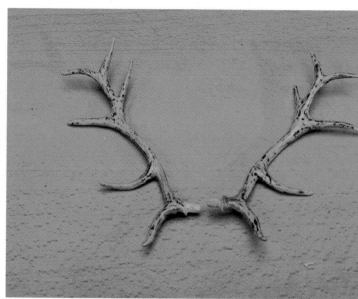

Here are the finished antlers

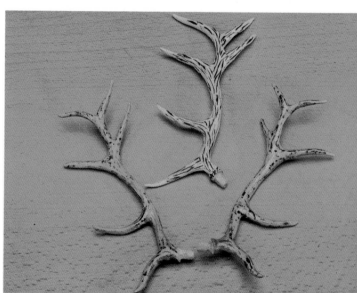

After the glue has dried, sand lightly with 320 sandpaper to smooth the surface and to give the antlers a horn-like feel.

Here are the finished antlers along with one before sanding and the application of Super Glue.

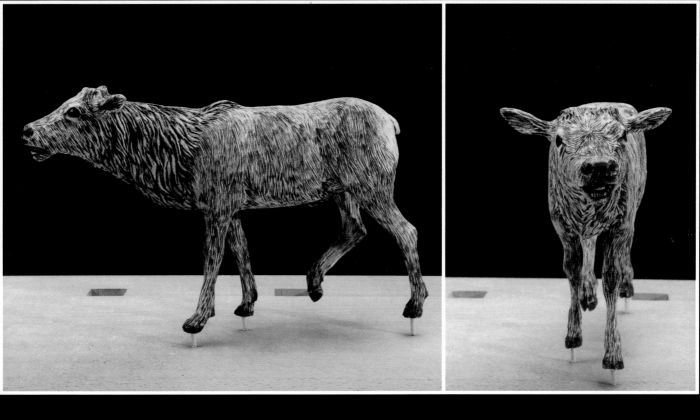

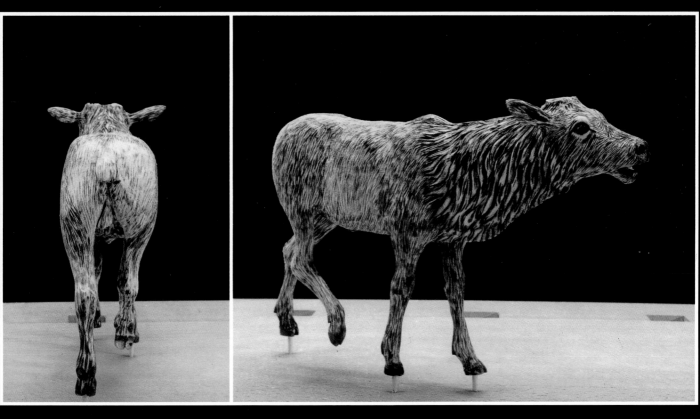

Here is how the elk should look after burning. He is ready for painting.

Painting the Elk

To paint the elk, use acrylic paints watered down enough so you could read through them to create washes of color. No animal is a solid color; the beauty of using the watered acrylics is that you may build up colors, allowing some to show through others in different places. The base color on the whole animal is a mixture of white and a very small amount of yellow ocher, just enough to change the white to a very light tan. Water down the mixed color and apply the watered base coat over the body and around the eyes. Do not use the undercoat on the ruff or along the outside of the ears which are the same color as the ruff. If you want examples of coloration and animal forms, the hunting and sporting magazines are always useful resources as are the children's nature magazines such as Ranger Rick, My Big Back Yard, and National Wildlife.

You can dry the paint quickly with a hair dryer.

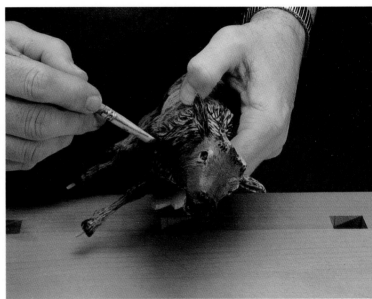

The ruff, the back of the ears and the face are painted VanDyke brown. Paint the face VanDyke brown.

Remember to put the base coat around the eyes. While most of the base coat will eventually be painted back out, some will show through around the eyes.

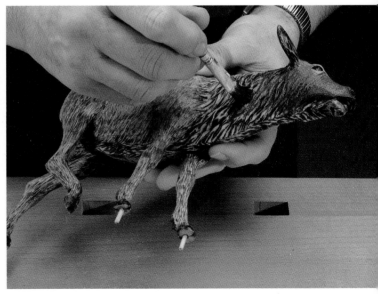

Paint the ruff VanDyke brown.

Paint the backs of the ears VanDyke brown.

The back legs are the color of the ruff from just above the bend in the leg down to the hoof.

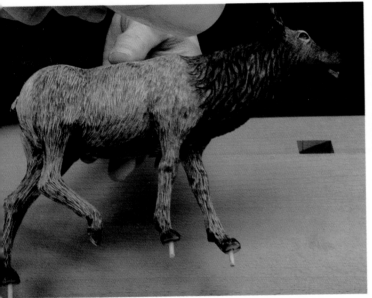

Dry the elk again. Notice the colors so far.

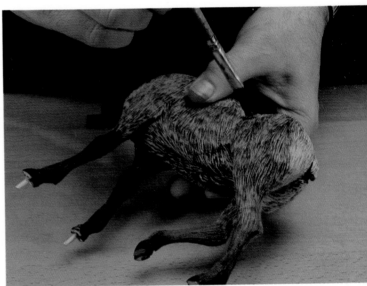

To blend the back leg color, just wet your brush and stroke the back leg color up over the hip.

Now we will paint the elk's legs. From about mid-calf on the front legs to the hoof use VanDyke brown again. Blend out the color where it changes to the body color to avoid any hard or sharp lines. To blend the leg color, just wet your brush and stroke the leg color up onto the shoulder.

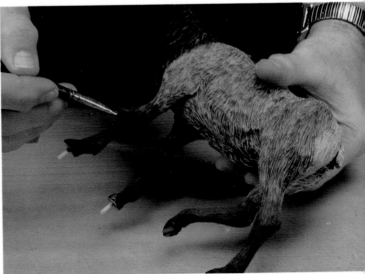

Put a second coat on the legs. They should be as dark if not darker than the ruff.

52

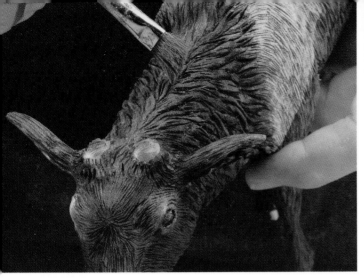

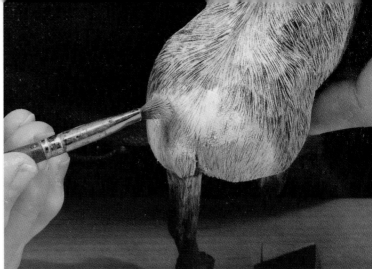

Lightly brush raw sienna down the center of the neck and between the horns on the forehead.

The color of the rump fades into the body in a broken line.

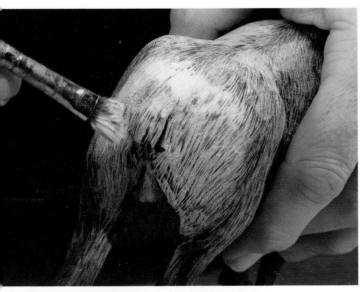

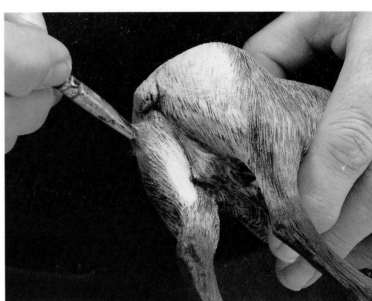

The rump color extends down the inside of the back legs on the upper inside area of the legs.

Now paint the rump, using white with just a little bit of the base coat added to it: just enough to take the starkness out of the white. Do not make this a solid line where it blends up into the body coat. It is a broken line.

Don't forget to do the insides of the ears with the base coat.

The teeth are white, watered down just a little bit to flow evenly.

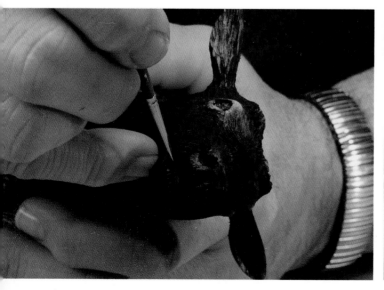

To paint the roof of the mouth use black paint without water. Leave the upper gum the color burning provided.

Paint the eyes black. At this scale pure black eyes will do.

Now paint the tongue red mixed with a lot of white to create a very light pink. You will not need much pink, this tongue is small.

Paint the nose black as well. Make sure the inside of the nostrils get painted.

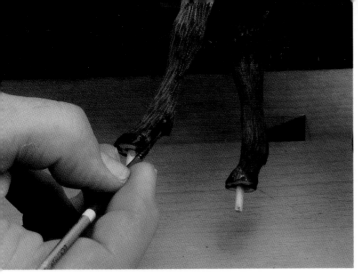

Paint the hooves and dewclaws black as well.

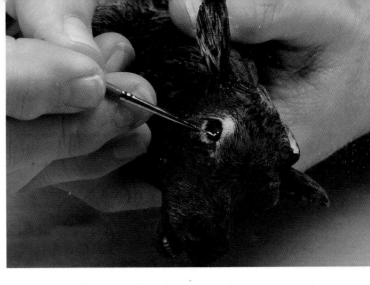

Add a little highlight in white to each eye.

Paint the underside of the raised hoof edge black.

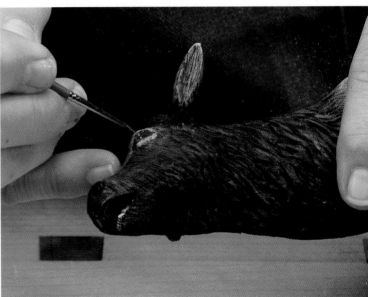

Add a clear gloss medium to the eyes now to give them a wet appearance.

Paint the inside of the raised hoof VanDyke brown.

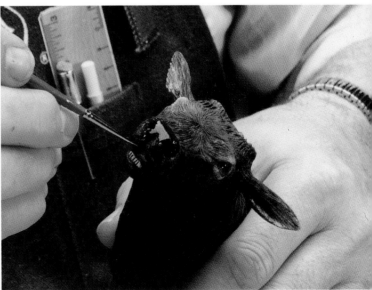

Add the clear gloss to the nose and tongue as well.

55

To paint the horns, use watered down VanDyke brown for all but the tips of the horns. Leave the tips unpainted; they are a lighter color. The tips will darken some when paste floor wax is applied later.

Now wax the horns. Rub the paste floor wax in with your finger tips. The horns are too small to apply the wax with a brush. Notice the change of the color in the tips of the horns

Supporting the horn with your hand, carefully brush the waxed horn with a soft bristled brush.

Now dry brush white over the elk to make all the highlights stand out. Always brush at 90 degrees to the hair. It makes the elk look like light is shining on him. It also ties the whole animal together. The white blends any heavy spots of color you may have into a whole, toning down differences.

Here are the waxed horns.

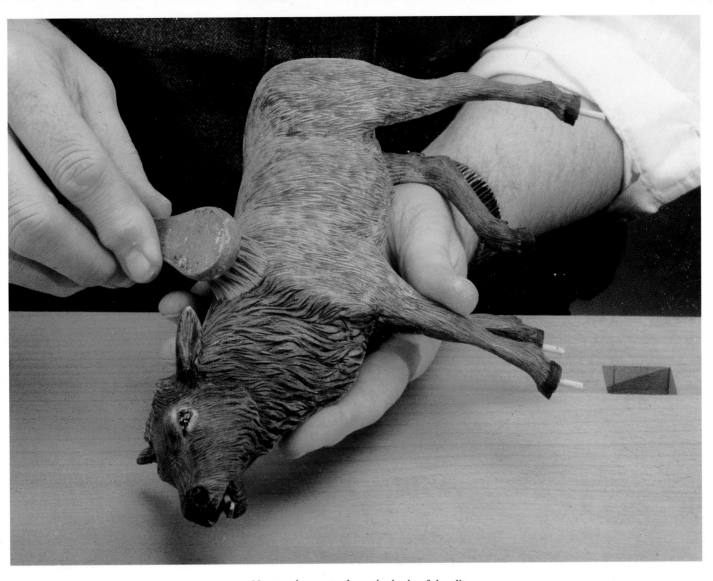

Now apply wax to the entire body of the elk.

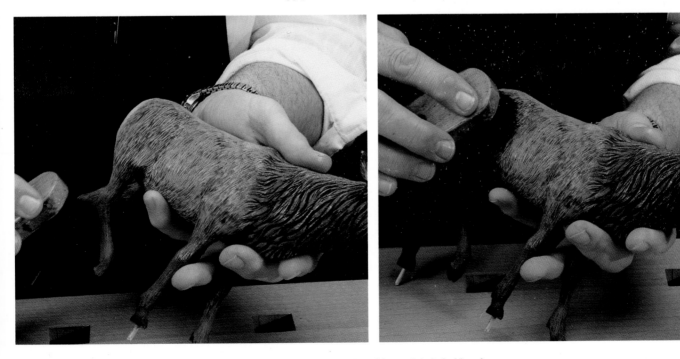

Brush down the waxed elk with a soft bristled brush.

Now glue the horns in place. Here is the finished elk with wooden pins in his hooves for mounting on a stand.

The stand itself can be fashioned into a habitat scene, assembling the rocks out of scraps taken from the carving.

The elk and the stand together for the finished look.

The Gallery

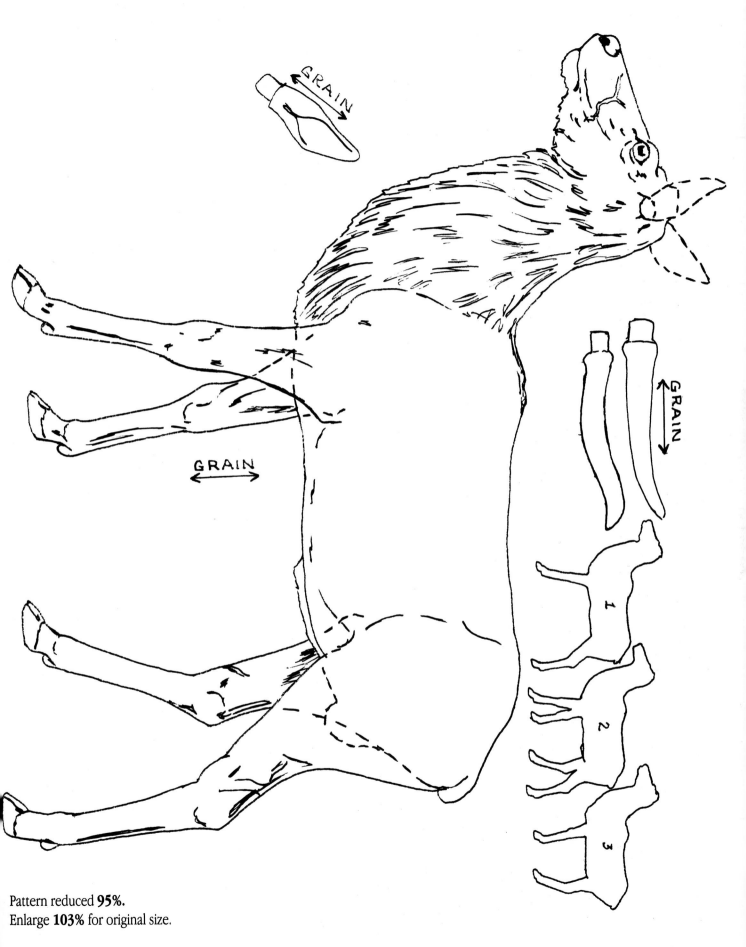

GRAIN

GRAIN

GRAIN

Pattern reduced **95%.**
Enlarge **103%** for original size.

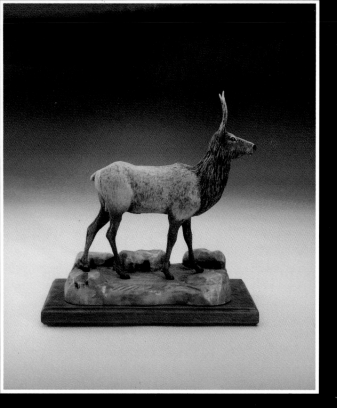

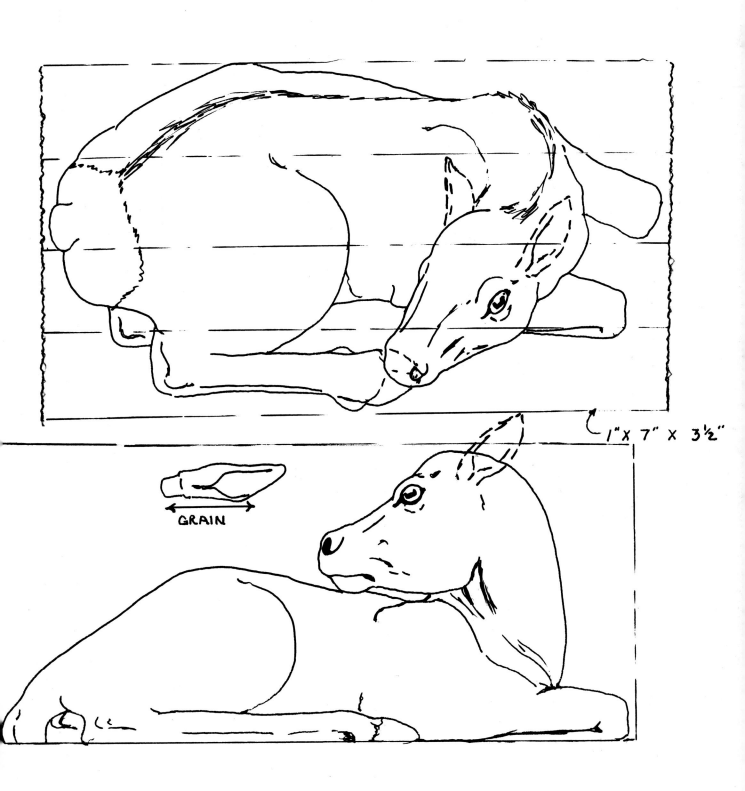

GRAIN

1" X 7" X 3½"

Pattern reduced **95%**.
Enlarge **103%** for original size.